THE CAT THAT PLAYED THE PIANO OUT OF TUNE

Kimberly A. Erb

authorHOUSE®

AuthorHouse™
1663 Liberty Drive
Bloomington, IN 47403
www.authorhouse.com
Phone: 1 (800) 839-8640

Published by AuthorHouse 05/26/2016

ISBN: 978-1-5246-0997-9 (sc)
ISBN: 978-1-5246-0996-2 (e)

Library of Congress Control Number: 2016908242

Print information available on the last page.

Any people depicted in stock imagery provided by Thinkstock are models,
and such images are being used for illustrative purposes only.
Certain stock imagery © Thinkstock.

This book is printed on acid-free paper.

Because of the dynamic nature of the Internet, any web addresses or links contained in
this book may have changed since publication and may no longer be valid. The views
expressed in this work are solely those of the author and do not necessarily reflect the
views of the publisher, and the publisher hereby disclaims any responsibility for them.

DEDICATION PAGE

I dedicate this book to God and Jesus. They help me write this book. And to my dad Ronald g Erb and mom Alice e Erb. They were the best parents in the world. And they gave me wings to fly. I will always love you. And to my sister Ronetta s Erb. Love you always. And Family and Friends thanks for being there. And all the Heroes of my book. They each have meant something to Me. And Gracie the cat and all my Pets with love Kimberly a Erb.

A pome called little house on the prairie. About Michael Landon. He came from a small Home town. Then he began to Rome. To be a Star someday. He hope and prayed. Did a show called Bonanza. Rode a horse. Of course. Called him little Joe. Who wouldn't know. Went on to do little House on the Prairie The Children called Him pa. He was the best of Them all. Did a show called Highway to Heaven. Where he was an Angel. Sent to make a different in People lives. To help Them survive. I was sad to here He was sick. I wish He would get better quick. He phot the good fight. But he lost His life. Good bye Michael Landon.

A pome called our veterans. There are Men and Women who join the military. They get sent Oversea. To fight for Liberty. They lay their Lives on the Line. So the World will be fine. Working hard to protect our Lands. Always giving a helping Hand. Spreading peace is what They do. For each and every one of You. War 1 war 2 Korea and Vietnam just to name a few. That's what They do. We lost so meany Men and Women. Sad but true. They died with Honor too. Some of Them get purple Harts. Because of what They did from the start. Every Veteran should be welcome Home. But when the Vietnam veterans come Home. They didn't get the welcome home they should've had. One of them was my Dad. I'm proud of what my Dad did in Vietnam. He was brave and Strong. I'm thankful for our Veterans everyday. There special in every way. So thank a Veteran today. I pray that there no more Wars for our Troops. God bless America. Here to our Veterans.

A pome called Dirty Dancing. About Patrick Swayze. There was a Boy who like to Dance. So He gave Ballet a chance. With his Mother as his Teacher. He reached for the Stars. And his Dreams came true. He got to be in a Movie too. It was called the Outsiders. But He was no outsider. He did a Movie Dirty dancing. Where He had everybody romancing. He sang a Song. To show He could do more. Then what was in Store. We thought He had a nice Life. With a good Wife. One day He was not Felling good. Like He should. Went to a Doctor. And He had Pancreatic cancer. He never let it slow Him down. He was always around. He fought like a Soldier. To win the War that was fighting against His Body. One night He lost the fight. I was sad that He was gone. Bet He showed the People He was strong. Stars are born. Heroes are made. So long Patrick Swayze.

A poem called I'm so glad We had this time together. About Carol Burnett. She was a funny Lady who could Sing. And do most anything. Me and my Mom saw Her on Tv. She made Us fans instantly. With Vicky Tim and Harvey and Lyle. They had such Style. Mama family was a hit. I got a lot out of it. She made Me laugh till my Trouble went away. That why I love Her to this day. I took a look at Her book too. And found out about People She knew. She did Movies. I like so much. Because She had a Magic touch. If I could meet Her one day. This is what I would say. I'm so glad We had this time together. Thanks Carol Burnett.

A poem about Ace. There this group I go with called Ace. They take Me to nice Places. Where I make new Friends. And the fun never ends. They help Me be a better Person. The Lady that pick Me up is nice and kind. She makes sure I have a good time. We played Bingo and go Bowling. And so meany other things. I'm glad to be in Ace. I wish Everybody could be in a group like Ace. Thank God for Ace. Now I get to go out. I would recommend Ace with out a doubt. Thanks Ace.

A poem called Step-Up. I go to a place called Step up. It a Safe place to go to. When your Happy or Blue. They know just what to do. Martina runs the place. And has a Pretty face. John is second in command. Alway lends a helping Hand. Nora comes by. To help give Us Wings to fly. We have a Boss named Ron. Who plays the Drums to Music and Song. The People have been though a lot. This is what They taught. When Life get tough and Hard to bear. Just remember Someone cares. I'm thankful for this place I go. I hope it will never Close. What will We do only God knows. Keep your Doors open and let People come in. Welcome them with a Smile and grin Step up.

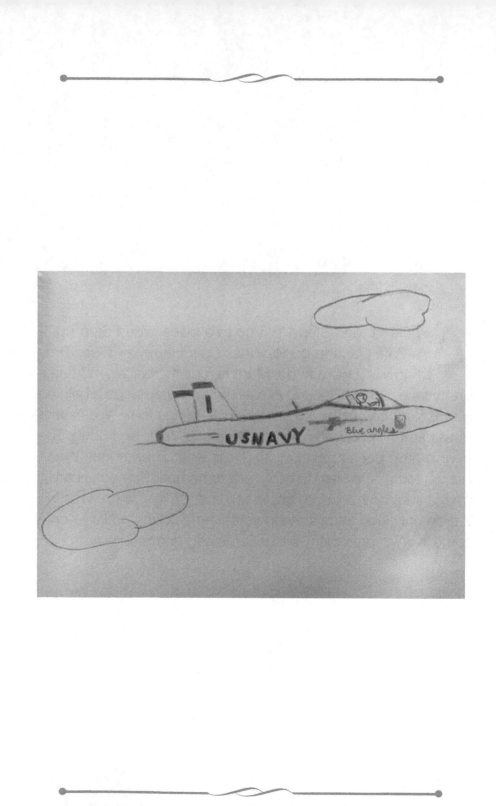

A poem called Angles in the sky. I heard loud noise. Looked in the Sky and saw the Blue angles go by. One two three or more. They were putting on a Show for sure. Beautiful as can be. Those Blue angles were a blessing for the People to see. There Planes were a pretty Blue. And They flue real fast too. They did fantastic Tricks in the Sky. I will remember Them till the day I Die. Spreading peace and good will is what They do. To show that the Military is there for more then just Wars too. Promoting the spirit of the USA. I hope that They will alway stay. Thanks for all You do for the Red White and Blue. And may God bless you Blue angles.

A poem called A voice of an angel. About Josh Groban. When He was a Boy cute as can be. Sang like an Angel for the World to see. He grew up to be the best person He could be. The special part was the Music came from his Hart. Songs like You raise me up and You are loved. Were written with care because He put his Feeling in them. He nice to his Fans. As he does his Concert across the Lands. I enjoyed Him on who do you think You are. When He found out about his Grandfather from afar. His Music means a lot to Me. When I'm down and out. His Music makes Me feel good without a doubt. Keep on Singing. Your Songs have a lot of meaning. I hope You have a wonderful Life. For all the joy you bring to Others. Keep sharing your gift with the World. For everyone should hear an Angel. Thanks Josh Groban.

A poem called captain jack. About Johnny Depp. When I first saw Johnny he was on 21 jump street. He was handsome to Me. And as special as can be. He had Talent greater then Anyone could believe. He had a lot to Achieve He did a movie Benny and Joon. He made Me swoon. What's eating Gilbert grape. I like that one too. In finding Never land. He had a plan. In Edward scissors Hands. He had helping Hands. In the movie Willy wonka. He was sweet. I enjoy Corpse bride. He was the Man voice from inside. I hope He dose more. Because I like Him for sure. Good luck Johnny Depp.

A pome called Big. About penny Marshall. A little Girl with big Dreams. So she though I can do Anything. She went on to do a Tv show called Laverne & Shirley. I liked seeing Her on Tv. Because she was a joy to Me. She travel around the World for a while. With Art gerfunkel because He made Her smile. Became a Director made Movies. She did a good Job on them from the start. Because she was Smart. Wrote a book. Gave us a special look at Her life. Witch I liked. She came along way. I like Her till this day. Was sick one Time. But now She fine. For all the joy you brought us Thanks penny.

A poem called my Rainforest friends. I have four Dart frogs. That are special and neat and so. Sweet. They are Cobalt blue tinctorius. Color like a Rainbow blue black yellow white and orange. Most dart frogs live in the Rainforest as you can see. But I got mine from the State of Tennessee. And they are not poisonous to Me. For The ones in the Rainforest are because of the Red ants they eat. The exo terra Terrarium is their Home. That's where They hop and roam. You save the Rainforest you save the Frogs. Conservation is the way to keep the Frogs here to stay. What the World needs is peace and Harmony in all living things. I see Gods beauty everywhere.

A pome called the flying none. About Sally Fields. She started out as Gidget And went on to be a None. That when She had fun. In Norma rae. She saved the day. She did the movie Places of the heart. She gave all Herself to the part. I liked her in Lincoln. She showed what a President wife was thinking. I loved her in Spiderman. She did all She can. I liked her on the Tv show Brothers and sisters. She was a great Mom. Who though them how to get along. I hope to get to see Her do more things. Because She swing. Have fun in what You do Sally Fields.

A pome our Tv friend. About Fred Rodgers. I had a Friend who was on the Tv each day. He taught Me how to act and Play. He took Me on a Trolley ride. To a we're a King reside. Mr mcfeely would bring things by. That we're Interesting to see. Picture picture on the Wall. Was the Greatest of them all. He had Fish big and small. And he like to Feed them all. He told Me that there only one Me. And he liked Me. He would Sing me Songs. That taught Me how to be Strong. I was Happy each day. when he came over to Play. I felt bad when He died. I knew there was a true Angle inside. I will remember Him everyday. He'll be my Hart in every way. So long old Friend Fred Rodgers.

Apome called the Music Man about Elton John. There was this Boy born with Music in his Blood. He learn to play the Piano and Sing. He love to do so Meany things. He wrote Songs from his Soul. It made Him feel whole. Song like Rocket man yellow brick road and Daniel. Shot Him to number one. I like the Music he did for the Movie the lion king. It make Me want to Sing. His Charity work far by none. The bust thing He ever done. He Touches so meany Lives. By his Actions not Words. He had some Painful things in his Life. But he a Fighter. I hope to see him in Concert one day I pray. Keep on making Music Elton John.

A pome called the band leader. About Lawrence Welk. There was a Show on Saturday nights. It was called the Lawrence Welk show. It was Something to know. He lead the Band. With a Stick in his Hand. Music he liked. It made him Feel right. Singing and Dancing did the trick. It gave Me such a Kick. He played an Accordion really well. It sounded Swell. He treated the Band members just like Family. And had Christmas with them on Tv. Here to a great Band leader Lawrence Welk.

A pome called I love Lucy. About Lucile Ball. There was this Lady who started out being Funny.!With big Dreams of Money. She did Movies and Tv shows. Everyone would knew Her were ever She goes. Me and my Mom liked seeing I love Lucy. We though is was so Fine. And she had a grate Mind. I love her Movie Yours mine and ours. I could Watch it for Hours. I liked her in the Movie Mame. It showed She had a lot of Fame. I saw Her on a Awards show Singing and Dancing with Michael Landon. It showed what true Stars they were. Here to a Funny lady Lucile Ball.

A pome called Those were the days. About Carol o Conner. There was a Man who wanted to be in Show business. He started to take Small parts. And Acted from his Hart. He did Movies and Tv shows. His jobs took Him to were ever he could go. I liked Him in All in the family. He sold the Show. By how much He node. he was good in the Heat of the night. It was such a Delight. I was Sad when His son died. He went after the Drug dealers that sold to His son. To make them Pay for what they done. And he Won. You were a good Man Carol o Conner.

A pome called Hello dolly. About Dolly Parton. There was a Little girl born in the Country. Music was a part of her Life. She went on to be Western music Star. Had a lot of Fans by far. Was on the Grand ole opry. She sang to her Harts content. She knew what this Meant. She did a Movie 9 to 5. She kept her Career alive. She built a Park. Called it Dolly wood. It would be better than Holly wood. I like the Tv show she did. When I was a Kid. She always Helps out when Someone in need. For that what She believes. Family matters the most to Dolly. Because they make her Happy and Jolly. Keep on singing Dolly Parton.

A pome called Soldier of love. About Donny Osmond. As a Kid cute as can be. And had a big Family. He sang with his Brothers. They were Like no others. They made a lot of Records for Us to buy. To give there Music a try. They had a Cartoon on Saturdays. It made Me happy always. They had a Tv show called the Donny and Marie show. it would make Me glow. He did the Music from the movie Mulan. It sound Beautiful and strong. He did a Talk show with his sister Marie. Me and my Mom liked it if you please. I'm glad He won Dancing with the stars. He put on the Best show by far. His family's had some Troubles. Yes it true. It was the Families glue that got them trough. You will always be my Soldier of love Donny Osmond.

A pome called Oklahoma. About Shirley Jones. There was this Blonde girl who grow up to be a Star. And She did a lot of things so Far. She made a Movie with Pat Boone. And became Famous real soon. She went on to do Partridge family. With Her step son David Cassidy. I like to hear her Sing and do most anything. She had some Trials. For a while but She kept her Smile. She had some Beautiful kids. She finally meant her Prince Charming. He was Funny and alarming. She has a Happy life now. She deserves it some how. Her Book was good. Just like I knew it would be. I wish You all the best Shirley Jones.

A pome called the skater. About Dorothy Hamill. There once was a Little girl who Dreamed of being a good Skater. She took Lessons as a Kid. And did all She did. She practices Jumping in the air. She had a Special flair. Won the Olympic gold. Because she was Bold. Had Cancer one day. That when I prayed. She Skated right trough it. I know She could do it. Saw her on Dancing with the stars. Dorothy has true Star quality. Has a Family that adore her. And so do I. Take care Dorothy Hamill.

A pome called Wonder Woman. About Linda Carter. There once a Little girl. Who grow up to be a Super hero. As Wonder Woman she won my Hart. Because She was the best part. She worked her Magic like Hero do. To save the World too. To Pretty for Words I could say. I enjoyed seeing Her on TV Wednesdays. As Wonder Woman She help me as a Kid. I believe I could do what She did. She had some Troubles in her life. She beat them because She a hero at Hart. I'm glad She has a better Life now. With her Son by Her side that how. Your a wonder Wonder Woman Linda Carter.

A pome called Let's get physical. About Olivia Newton John. There was this Cute little girl. That grew into a Wonderful woman. She stared in a Movie called Greece with a Guy named John. And she went into Dance and Song. She was Fantastic as can be. For all the People to see. I love her in Xanadu. Because all She could do. I watched it so many times on Tv. It Means so much to Me. I was sad to here She had Cancer. She was a Trooper and got trough it. Because She had the Hart to do it. She works with Cancer foundation. Hoping for a cure. God bless you Olivia Newton John.

A pome called Here's Jonny about Jonny Carson. There once was a Guy who did a Talk show. He did it late at Night. And He did it all right. He made you Feel like part of his Family. When you were watching Him on Tv. He was Nice and kind. And had a Sharp mind. He talked to the People we Liked the most. Because he was a Good host. His Comedy skits were a hit. They were so Cute. We liked them to Boot. I was sad when He was not on Tv any more. I thought He had much more in Store. He could never be Replace. And we Miss his Smiling face. Here's to Jonny.

A pome call the Puppet master. About Jim Henson. There once was a Man who made Puppets. And He called them his Muppets. With Kermit and Fozzie the Bear and all the rest. He gave the People his very best. He went to Work for Sesame Street. Because He was so Neat. He once made a Lion that look so Real. You thought he'll Eat you for his Meal. His Movies were so Bold. They touch the Young and the Old. It was Sad to lose a Man. That had Wonderful plans. He went to Heaven far away. To put on more Puppets plays. We will never forget Him or his Characters. And jest like Kermit said in a book. That He miss his Friend Jim. And We do too. Farewell Jim.

A pome called We all need hope. About Bob Hope. There once was a cute Baby boy born. On one Sunny morn. He grew up to be a Movie star. And drove a Sports car. He made Movies with a Guy named Bing. They would do Anything. On the Weekends when He was off. He went to play Golf. I like his Network specials on Tv. Because they meant a lot to Me. He put on Shows for are Troops in other Countries. To thank Them for Fighting for the Land of the Free. Thanks for giving Us hope Bob hope.

A pome called Walk like a man. About Howie Mandel. First Job he had was in Carpet retail. But He had no Sales. Then became a Doctor on TV. But didn't make House calls to Me. When I saw his Movie walk like a Man. I became his biggest Fan. America got talent I like to see. Because of Howie. His Comedy is just Swell. It makes me feel Well. I learned a lot from his Book. He took a Special look. At Mental illness from the Start. It was something He knew in his Hart. I'm glad He came out about what He had. It made a lot Mentally ill People glad. I'm proud of you Howie Mandel.

A pome called The divine Miss m. About Beth Midler. Everywhere she goes. People talk about her Movie the Rose. She noticed for Meany things. We like to Hear her Sing. She come a Long way. Sense her Early days. I liked her Movie beaches. It had a lot to Teach us. Her song the Wind beneath my wings. Makes me Grateful for many Things. Her personality is Neat. Because she Sweet. She has a nice Family. And there Proud of Her. Here to you Beth Midler.

A pome called The woman who stood the Test of time about Cher. When I first saw Cher she was with Sonny. And she was Warm and Funny. She could Sing and Act. And do a lot of Things in fact. I liked her Show. I wished it didn't have to Go. She went on to become a Megastar And took her Career far. With movies Mask and Burlesque. She did her Best. But Music is in her Blood. For that her first Love. She tried to help People everywhere She goes. Because it keep Her on her Toes. I was glad when She said she liked the Eights. For I do too. Keep turning Back time Cher.

pome called Life is like a box of chocolates. About Tom Hanks. When Tom Hanks was on a show with Peter Scolari. I know he would be a big Star. And go Far. He was a Class act. For a Fact. In Forrest Gump he was a Good guy. Who gave Everything a try. His Talent is Like no other. He got it from his Father and Mother. He works so Hard on everything from the Start. Because he has a good Hart. Everybody wants to be his Friend. Because he there for Them till the End. I liked Cloud atlas. Nothing could Match it. I hope and Pray. That I will meet Him someday. But for Now. I say thanks Tom Hanks.

A pome called The Grate skate. About Scott Hamilton. I know a Guy who could Skate. And could do Figure eights. He was so Fast on his Feet. He couldn't be Beat. He went to the Olympics games. After the Games his Life was not the same. He put on a Lot of Shows. For every One to know. you could Go on with a Show. He did Backflips on the Ice. They were Cool and Nice. I herd One day he was Sick. It made me sad real Quick. I'm glad He has a Wife. And two Beautiful kids in his Life. Scoot you are a Hero to Me. With everything You been Through. You still have More to Do. We love you Scott Hamilton.

A pome about Mary Tyler Moore. There once was a Lady name Mary Tyler Moore. Who gave Us so much more. She started on a Tv show. For everyone to know what an Actress she is. She did a Show with Guy name Dick. That did the Trick. One day she went to a Hospital real quick. Because she was Sick. They told Her she had Diabetes tip One not two. And then They said here what You do. She realized something She could do. To help People with One and two. She helped the Juvenile diabetes foundation. So there won't be a next's Diabetes generation. I read her Book too. And it made Me feel like She know. How I felt about having Diabetes too. I thank God for you Mary Tyler Moore.

A pome called When you Wish upon a Star. About Walt Disney. There once was a Dreamer who dream Grate things. That I never Seen. He took us to Places near and Fare. By wishing on a Star. He gave Us a Mouse to see. He came into our Homes on TV. He had so Meany idea and Plans. That he Build a Wonder land. We're kids Young and Old can go. To Hear story Untold. We're fairy Teals do come True. For Everyone who Believes in them too. His Movies were Grate. They take the Cake. With Tinker bell by His side. He took Us on Magical ride. Why He had to Go. I don't know. God most thought He need a Rest because He gave Us his Best. The World will never be the Same with out Walt Disney.

A pome called Straight talk and comedy. About Whoopi Goldberg. I like Whoopi Goldberg she so Neat. She knocks Me off my Feet. She a good Comedian from the Start. She put in all her Hart. The movie Ghost was a big Hit. Because She was in it. I love to Hear her Straight talk. I could Hear it around the Clock. She started Live aid with the Help of her Friends Billy and Robin. To do all She can for the People across the Land. She bright Beautiful and Bold. And she never get Old. I wish I could Speak like Her and say what on my Mind. And do it all the Time. Your One of a kind Whoopi Goldberg.

A pome called. The Man behind Peanuts. About Charles Schulz. There once was Man who Drew comics. From the Start with his Hart. In the Beginning he called them Little folks. But They were no Jokes. Charlie Brown and Snoppy and the Gang. They still Today remain the Same. There was a Kite eating Tree. Where Charlie Brown tried to Set his Kite free. Where Schroeder liked Beethoven to much. That he Played his Stuff. Lucy thought She was Miss know it all. But Didn't Show it all. Linus setting in a Pumpkin patch. Waiting for his Halloween bag of Joy. Snoopy came Home from Fighting the Red Baron. Wood stalk would ask how He was Faron. One day God took Charles Schulz away. He needed another Angle that Day. We will alway Remember you. And your Characters too. We Love you Charles Schulz.

A pome about my cat Gracie Elaine. Would you think of that. I have a Cat. Cute as can be. And she loves Me. She likes watching Movies and Tv shows. And she fallow me everywhere I go. When I'm sick she alway there. Because she Cares. She American short hair. Fluffy like a Bear. I read her Books. When she in Her special Nook. That is my Lap. We're she sometimes takes a Nap. She play with String And almost anything. God sent her from Heaven above. So she could give Me her Love. Everyone should go and adopt a Pet from a Shelter to. Because you'll have Someone there for You. Even when your Blue. I love you Gracie Elaine.

Sadly Today we lost a Icon. the Pillsbury doughboy Died. At the age of 49 at the Backer joy Hospital. He died of Complications do to a Yeast infection. He was Survived by his wife Cinnamon roll and his two Kids his daughter Crescent and Son biscuit. His body was taken to the Betty corker Funeral home. Instead of being fell with Formaldehyde. They felled him with Grape jelly. They will Roast him at 350 for 1 Hour. Officiating at his Funeral was hostess Twinkie. The company Spokes woman said he had Hot cross buns. He will be Buried at the Cake boss cemetery. And on his Tomb stone it will Read. May you Rise to meet the grate Baker in the Sky. With the money Cinnamon roll received. She went to get Breast implants. But all She got were two Cup cakes. The Moral of the Story is I never Meant a Doughnut I didn't Like.

A pome called English rose. About Princess Diana. There once was a English rose who lived in London. She was Pretty and Fair. And showed the People she Cared. She married a Prince. To be a Princess. And a grate Princess she was. Everywhere she went She touched so many Lives. By her Generosity. She had a Special philosophy. To spread Good will across the Land. To alway be a Helping hand. She had two Beautiful boys. They were her Pride and Joy. Though she didn't Live a Fairy tale life. She took in all in Stride. I was Shocked and Sadden. When we Lost our English rose. She will alway Be the People princess. We will not for get her Style and Grace. And her Beautiful face. We will Miss her Always and forever princess Diana.

A pome about Robin Williams. The Tears be hind the Laughter. There wants was a Man who could make People laugh. In till We fell on to our Backs. He had so many Gifts to Share. That he Shared them with the World that Cared. He believe in Helping others. No matter if They were not his Sister or Brothers. But behind his Smile was Sadness and Pain. For He had a Broken hart that Remained. He tried to get Better. But the Pain didn't go Alway. So that why He Killed himself One day. I cried The day He died. Because he didn't Survive. Now may He rest in peace. Somewhere beyond the Clouds in the Sky. For that were Angles go when they Die. I will Miss him for the Rest of my Life. He taught Me it was ok to be Funny. And that Laughter is the Best medicine. Goodby Robin.

A pome About 9 11. I woke up to the Sound of the Tv. I couldn't Believe my Eyes. I thought it was a Dream but it was True. Plane one and Plane two Flew into the Twin towers. jest like They were Meant to do. A short Time later a Plane flew into the Pentagon. I thought There must be Something wrong. Then flight 93 that was Meant to Crash into the Capital in Washington, D.C. Instead went Down in Pa. A Fear came over Me. I didn't Feel like I was Living in the Land of the Free. The Mayer of New York went right to the Twin towers. He looked for Peoples body's for Hours. He stayed there all Night and till Morning light. To make sure that the People of New York would be all Right. With the Police and Fire department by his side. They tried to Save so many Lives. Another hero was a Catholic priest. Who went into a Tower. To Pray for God divine power. The Tower fell upon Him and he Died. Showing what a True priest he was Inside. Thanks to the Navy seals for getting the Terrorist. So we could have Peace at last. We will alway Remember 9 11. And God bless America.

A pome called Behind the crystal Ball. About Billy Crystal. There once was a Man who was Funny. So he Tried to make Money. He worked on a show <u>Saturday night</u> live. To See if his Career would Survive. He made a Movie in search of Curly gold. Which I thought was Bold. With His friend Robin. He kept Billy hopping. Billy Crystal cared about the People in his Life. Especially his Family and his Wife. With out a Doubt. He always Helping someone Out. I will alway Remember the tribute. He did on his friend Robin. To a Good guy Billy Crystal.

A pome called Little Miss dimples. About Shirley Temple. Little miss dimples Cute as can be. Was a Famous movie Star at age Three. Little miss Dimple we Love you. She sang and Dance to a Happy little Tune. Her Mom curled her Hair each Night. So she would Look jest Right. She tug at our Hart strings with her Smile. That We for got our Troubles for a While. She saved a Studio from Bankruptcy. By being the Best star She could be. She became Ambassador to the United nations. To spread Peace and Good will to Everyone. I was Sad when she died. God needed another Angle by his Side. I will Remember her Sweet face. Here's to you Shirley temple.

A pome called. Back to the future. About Michael j Fox. He was a Man from the Past. With plans for the Future. He was on Family ties. And he was a Nice surprise. I like his Movies they were Good. He did Everything an Actor would. He made me Laugh and made me Cry. Because he is a Super guy. I was glad when he Married the Girl of his Dreams. I thought his Life would be Serene. He had some Sweet kids. That were Pretty neat. One day a Gray cloud rolled over his Head. It give him Fear and Dread. He woke up not Feeling like him Self. He wonder what He should do for him Self. So he went to a Doctor one Day. To see what the Doctor had to Say. He said it was Parkinson's disease. That made Michael feel not at Ease. I like Reading his Books. He show what his Life is Like now. And how Things matter some How. He started a Foundation for Parkinson's disease. Looking for a Cure if you Please. I hope he Finds a Cure one Day. So no One will have to Suffer the same way. Your My hero Michael j fox.

A pome called A Golden girl. About Betty white. When I first saw Betty White. She was a Delight. She knew how to make Money. By being Funny. She had a Nice life. And made a Good wife. I enjoy the Tv shows she made. They will never Fade. She became an Animal rights Activists. And said that Everyone should have a Best friend. She wrote a Cute book about her Self. To show that there was No one Else. She an Inspiration to Me. She keeps Working in her Ninety. You'll alway be Golden to me Betty white.

A pome called The Son of God. A long time ago a Baby boy was born. He was God son. An only One. He went into a Temple to talk to a Priest. About God bountiful Feast. He went to a Wadding one Time. And turn Water into Wine. On a Boat in the Roaring seas. He calm The seas as he Pleased. He walk on Water. Like no other. He healed the Sick. And Help them real Quick. Nulled to a Tree. To set are Souls free. He Rose from the Dead. That what the Bible said. He went to Heaven to set on his Throne. God his Father would not be Alone. Thank you God for sending your son Jesus.

A pome called I write the songs. About Barry Manilow. There once was a Man who spread his Music across the Land. With a Small band. He played his Piano to a Lovely tune. It made you Feel better real soon. Songs like Mandy and I am your child. He would make you Smile. He showed the World what a Good guy He was. By how He acted from Inside. He made Songs for Movies. I thought they were Groovy. I got his Records and a Eight track tape too. Because He was Cool. God gave him his Gift of Music. For Us to enjoy. I hope to see One of his Shows. Before I go. I would Like to Thank him for all He did. His Music help Me get though Tuff times when I was a Kid. Thank you Barry manilow.

Poem about my hero Christopher Reeves. when I went to see him on the Big screen. He was the best thing I ever seen. He flew into my Hart never to Depart. I could tell by his sparkly Blue eyes. He was a Angel in disguise. He made a difference to Me. And the World to see. He was stronger then most Men. His greatest Muscle was his Hart. His actions spoke louder then Words. That I ever herd. His smile lit up a Room. And made People fell better real soon. His generosity. Was His philosophy. With fist of Steel. He had Determination and will. With power Love and light. He phot with all His might. He tried to be a Superman. And do all He can. He tried to save the People like Heroes do. By starting the Christopher and Diana Reeves foundation too. He had faith that He would walk one day. That when We all started to pray. Oh why did He die. When he was a super Guy. He set the example for Us to fallow. Because He was a Good fellow. His books were an inspiration to Me. To be the best person I could be. Jest like the Superman song by Five for fighting it not easy. It was not easy for Christopher Reeves. He will be Remember. And not Forgotten. I was sad when his wife Diana died eighteen Months later.

A pome called My Mother Alice.
My Mother is so sweet. She can't be Beat.
God made her with Special care. So she could be there for Me.

She was Like nobody Else. Because she was always Her self.

She taught Me about love life and Laughter. Because she wanted Me to have a Happily ever after.

She got Cancer one day. And she phot to Stay but had to go away. I miss till this Day. Cherish your Mother. Because you won't get Another.

I was Blessed to have what I had. Everyday she made me glad. So hug your Mother today. Before she goes Away.

Say you love her too. I think about you Mom from the Start. Because you always Remain in my Hart. I will always Love you no matter what I do. Until the Day I can be with You. Love Kim.

A poem I called the decade that last forever. All about the Eights. The Eights rock and roll. Had a lot of Soul. The Music videos were special from the start. Till this day they remain in my Hart. The Video games true to there names. Like PAC man Donkey kong Mario brothers Galaga Centpede They were fun to play. I wished I could played them all day. The Movies meant a lot to me like. Superman Star wars Ghostbuster Et. They got everybody wanting to go to the Movies. The Tv shows like Happy days Mork and mindy and Days of our lives. They were a joy to Me. I love watching them on Tv. The toys I had Gameboy Speck & spell Care Bears and Little professor Cabbage patch doll. They were the best Toys of them all. The 80 were a special decade to Me. That decade will never Die. Because of the Magic it had. It made those Ten years of my life not fill so bad. Here's to the 80.

Printed in the United States
By Bookmasters